# SUPERSTARS
## of
# PRO
# FOOTBALL

DESEAN JACKSON

## Seth H. Pulditor

**Mason Crest Publishers**
Philadelphia

MASON CREST PUBLISHERS, INC.
370 Reed Road
Broomall PA 19008
(866) MCP-BOOK (toll free)
www.masoncrest.com

Printed in the United States of America.

CPISA compliance information: Batch#060110-FB3. For further information, contact Mason Crest Publishers at 610-543-6200.

First printing

9 8 7 6 5 4 3 2 1

Library of Congress Cataloging-in-Publication Data

Pulditor, Seth H.
  DeSean Jackson / Seth H. Pulditor.
      p. cm. — (Superstars of pro football)
  Includes bibliographical references and index.
ISBN 978-1-4222-1663-7 (hc)
ISBN 978-1-4222-1983-6 (pb)
 1. Jackson, DeSean, 1986—Juvenile literature. 2. Football players—United States—Biography—Juvenile literature.  3. Philadelphia Eagles (Football team)—Biography—Juvenile literature.  I. Title.
GV939.J26P85 2010
796.332092—dc22
[B]                                                              2010000362

Publisher's note:
All quotations in this book come from original sources and contain the spelling and grammatical inconsistencies of the original text.

## ◀◀ CROSS-CURRENTS ▶▶

In the ebb and flow of the currents of life we are each influenced by many people, places, and events that we directly experience or have learned about. Throughout the chapters of this book you will come across CROSS-CURRENTS reference bubbles. These bubbles direct you to a CROSS-CURRENTS section in the back of the book that contains fascinating and informative articles and related pictures. Go on. ▶▶

# ◀◀ CONTENTS ▶▶

# A TASTE OF THINGS TO COME

September 7, 2008, was a gorgeous day in Philadelphia, with sunny skies and mild temperatures. For fans of the Eagles, Philadelphia's National Football League (NFL) **franchise**, the lovely weather was just a bonus. This was opening day of the 2008 season, and nothing could have dampened the enthusiasm of the Eagles' faithful.

Hours before the 1:00 P.M. start of the game, crowds had gathered in the parking lots surrounding Lincoln Financial Field. Expectations ran high. After a disappointing 2007 season, Philadelphia's famously passionate football fans were desperate to see their team return to its winning ways.

No one knew what to expect from rookie DeSean Jackson before his first professional football game in September 2008. Although the young player had blazing speed, he was smaller than most players in the National Football League (NFL). Could the quick wide receiver become an impact player for the Philadelphia Eagles?

## "Let's Add Some Weapons"

In the six seasons preceding the 2007 campaign, the Philadelphia Eagles had finished first in the National Football Conference (NFC) East Division five times. They had reached the playoffs five times, advancing all the way to the Super Bowl, the NFL's championship game, in the 2004 season. But in 2007 the team had stumbled to an 8–8 record, finishing dead last in the NFC East and missing the playoffs entirely.

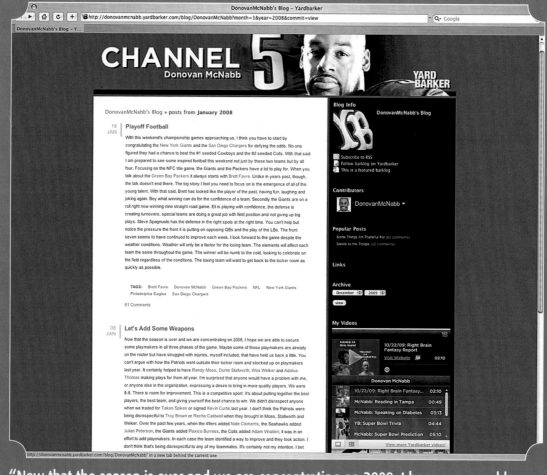

"Now that the season is over and we are concentrating on 2008, I hope we are able to secure some playmakers," Eagles quarterback Donovan McNabb wrote in his blog on January 8, 2008. "This is a competitive sport. It's about putting together the best players, the best team, and giving yourself the best chance to win."

After that dismal season, Eagles quarterback Donovan McNabb had stirred up a minor controversy by publicly calling on the team to acquire some big playmakers. Such players have the explosive speed, dazzling moves, or exceptional athletic ability to turn a routine play into a huge one.

**CROSS-CURRENTS**

For a profile of quarterback Donovan McNabb, who has been leading the Philadelphia Eagles' offense since 1999, see page 46.

The Eagles' 2007 roster boasted one such game-changing weapon: running back Brian Westbrook. Rushing and receiving, Westbrook had gained a total of 2,104 yards, best in the NFL. Wide receiver Kevin Curtis had also posted a solid season, catching 77 passes for 1,110 yards. But Curtis—whom the Eagles had acquired as a **free agent** after the 2006 season—was the Eagles' top receiver, and he scored just 6 touchdowns. By contrast, as McNabb noted in a post on his blog titled "Let's Get Some Weapons," the New England Patriots had added free agent wide receivers Randy Moss and Wes Welker to their team after the 2006 season. In 2007, the speedy Welker scored 8 touchdowns, a pair more than the Eagles' Curtis. Moss had a league-leading 23 TD receptions, just one fewer than the number for all the Eagles *combined*.

Not coincidentally, the Patriots compiled a 16–0 record during the 2007 regular season and made it to the Super Bowl. McNabb insisted that he meant no disrespect to any of his teammates, but he said,

**❝We were 8–8. There is room for improvement.❞**

Philadelphia Eagles team management has a reputation for avoiding controversy. While McNabb's comments generated a buzz on local sports radio, head coach Andy Reid, team president Joe Banner, and owner Jeffrey Lurie had little to say publicly about the matter. Nor did the Eagles address their quarterback's desire for more "weapons" by trading for or signing as a free agent a big-name wide receiver. They didn't even use a top pick in the 2008 draft to select a wide receiver from the ranks of college players. After trading away their first-round pick and

**CROSS-CURRENTS**

The NFL's annual draft is the method by which teams select new players from the ranks of college football. For more information on the draft, turn to page 47.

drafting defensive tackle Trevor Laws, the Eagles finally selected—with the 49th overall pick of the draft—a wide receiver from the University of California. His name was DeSean Jackson.

Few people who followed college football would deny that DeSean Jackson was an exciting player. He had great speed and flashy moves. In the open field, he was hard to catch. But at 5'10" tall and weighing only 167 pounds, he was undersized for an NFL receiver. Many football analysts doubted that DeSean would be able to run routes over the middle, where big linebackers deliver big hits. They also thought that pro cornerbacks would be able to jam DeSean at the line of scrimmage. This would neutralize his speed, stop him from getting deep downfield on pass routes, and ultimately prevent him from becoming the kind of offensive playmaker that Donovan McNabb believed the Eagles needed.

In preseason games, DeSean had shown flashes of brilliance, including a 76-yard punt return for a touchdown. But there is a world of difference between the preseason—when final scores don't matter and the top players are used sparingly—and the regular season. As they filed into Lincoln Financial Field for the 2008 regular-season opener, against the St. Louis Rams, Philadelphia fans were anxious to see whether the rookie wide receiver from Cal could perform when it counted.

## Big Debut

It didn't take long to find out, and the Eagles' faithful were not disappointed. On just the second play from scrimmage, Donovan McNabb dropped back and looked to his right, where DeSean Jackson and Rams cornerback Tye Hill were racing down the sideline. Hill had excellent coverage, but McNabb decided to throw to DeSean anyway. The ball floated 25 yards from the line of scrimmage. In full stride, DeSean jumped over the defender to catch the pass, then ran for about 20 more yards before finally being dragged down. The play, which went for 47 yards, set up the Eagles' first touchdown. Philadelphia never looked back, demolishing St. Louis, 38–3.

St. Louis Rams cornerback Tye Hill tries to stop DeSean Jackson (# 10) after a catch during the 2008 season-opening game, September 7, 2008. DeSean's six catches, as well as his spectacular effort returning punts, helped the Eagles defeat the Rams, 38 to 3.

DeSean led all receivers in the game with six passes for 106 yards. It was the first time in five years that a rookie wide receiver had gained more than 100 yards in his first NFL game. DeSean also contributed to Philadelphia's blowout victory with an exciting punt return. Although he didn't score, the 60-yard return was nearly twice as long as the longest punt return the Eagles had gotten in 2007. Clearly, DeSean Jackson was going to add a big-play dimension to the Eagles' offense.

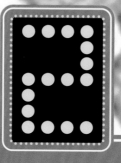

# EARLY YEARS

**D**eSean Jackson was born in Long Beach, California, on December 1, 1986. He was the fifth child of Gayle and Bill Jackson, who would have two more kids after DeSean. In the large Jackson family, sports were emphasized. This was especially true for DeSean and his four brothers.

Their father had been an outstanding athlete during his youth in Pittsburgh, Pennsylvania. A high school track star, Bill Jackson had run the 100-meter dash in a speedy 10.4 seconds. He dreamed of playing football in the NFL. Unfortunately, his family was poor and could not afford to send Bill to college. The family also considered his dreams of a pro sports career foolish

DeSean Jackson grew up in the Los Angeles area. Located in Southern California, the "City of Angels" has a population of more than 3.5 million, making it the second-largest city in the United States.

and impractical. After high school, Bill went to work in a steel mill. Later, when hard times hit the steel industry, he found a job as a streetcar driver. Eventually, Bill and Gayle Jackson decided to move to California to raise their family. They settled in a neighborhood in central Los Angeles.

## Practicing with Pops

Though his dreams of a pro football career had been thwarted, Bill Jackson hoped that his sons might have a chance to play in the NFL. He drove his boys continually to practice throwing and catching a football. He drilled them in how to run crisp pass patterns. Of her husband, Gayle Jackson would recall,

**"Oh, he pushed them. I think he pushed them very hard. To the point sometime where they even questioned themselves. 'What if I really didn't want to do this?'"**

For the oldest Jackson son, Byron, the demanding training sessions paid off. Byron played wide receiver at San Diego State University. He also made it to the NFL, though in his two seasons with the Kansas City Chiefs he never made it off the **practice squad.**

As gifted an athlete as Byron was, Bill Jackson recognized early on that DeSean was in a different class entirely. DeSean, who is 18 years younger than Byron, showed remarkable speed, quickness, and **hand-eye coordination** before he'd even entered kindergarten. And he shared his father's dreams. The young DeSean wanted nothing more than to become a pro football player. By the age of five, he was spending several hours each week running pass patterns under his father's watchful eye. On Sundays during football season, the two watched the NFL games together. Bill Jackson would always take the opportunity to explain some of the finer points of the game. He would, for example, show DeSean how a receiver had beaten the zone defense, or explain why the quarterback had made the wrong decision by throwing into **double coverage**.

## Family Breakup

DeSean and his father were extremely close. So it could have come as a devastating blow to the boy when his parents split up. The divorce occurred when DeSean was only six. Fortunately, Bill and Gayle Jackson both felt strongly that their children needed two parents. They stayed on friendly terms after the breakup. And Bill remained very involved in his kids' lives. In fact, throughout much of his childhood, DeSean would live with his father, who had a small apartment in the South Los Angeles neighborhood of Crenshaw. DeSean would always appreciate his father's involvement in his life. He later noted:

Despite his small size, DeSean was good enough to star at Long Beach Polytechnic High School—no small accomplishment, considering that in 2005 *Sports Illustrated* rated the school's athletic program first among the nation's 38,000 high schools. Here DeSean, wearing #1, returns the opening kickoff during a 2004 game against Lakewood High.

**❝A lot of my friends didn't really have two parents. A lot of them only had mothers. To have that father relationship, there's nothing like it. . . . That's your buddy. You're doing everything together.❞**

If they didn't really do *everything* together, DeSean and his father certainly did a lot together. Sports continued to be the focus of many of their activities. As DeSean became involved in organized youth athletics, Bill Jackson drove him to practices and games. Whenever DeSean was on the field, Bill would be on the sidelines or in the stands. He was usually the loudest person in attendance. "I had the craziest Pops," DeSean would remember fondly.

Beyond his own passion for sports, Bill Jackson believed it was important to keep his son busy and focused on future goals. Crenshaw is a gritty neighborhood. Bill didn't want DeSean learning bad lessons and getting into trouble on the streets. That was a concern Gayle Jackson also shared. She noted:

**"Football was important for my son in just about every way, really. He learned so much about respecting others, being positive and building character."**

## Rough Teachers

Throughout his elementary and middle school years, DeSean Jackson dominated the competition in every youth football league in which he played. None of the other kids could match his blazing speed. By the time DeSean turned 14, neither could his brother Byron, who only a few years earlier had been faster than any other player for the Kansas City Chiefs.

After his brief stint in the NFL, Byron had become a video editor and film producer. He used his skills to document virtually every athletic competition in which his younger brother participated, beginning when DeSean was about seven. Byron even videotaped DeSean's workouts. He also helped supervise DeSean's training. In this Byron was joined by three college football teammates.

The men were rough **mentors**. DeSean was small, but when defending him in a practice session, they didn't hesitate to push him around. DeSean was also very confident, and Byron's friends took it upon themselves to make sure he didn't become too cocky. A practice videotaped by Byron following DeSean's graduation from eighth grade was typical. The youngster—all 5'2" and 110 pounds of him—runs pass routes, covered closely by one of the burly adults. Though DeSean effortlessly hauls in catch after catch, the men keep up a stream of taunts:

**"They say you aren't good enough, aren't big enough, aren't tough enough. You'll never play at Long Beach Poly."**

## High School Sensation

Long Beach Polytechnic High School has long been renowned for its athletic programs—in particular, its football teams, which have produced more NFL players than any other high school in the country. In 2000, Bill Jackson moved from Los Angeles to Long Beach, a city of about 460,000 located some 20 miles south of downtown L.A., so that DeSean would have a chance to play for Poly.

**CROSS-CURRENTS**

In 2005, *Sports Illustrated* named Long Beach Polytechnic the "Sports School of the Century." To find out why, turn to page 48.

DeSean made the most of the opportunity. He was indeed good enough and tough enough to play at Poly. And, over the course of his high school years, he grew, standing 5'9" tall and weighing about 160 pounds by his senior season. While this by no means made DeSean huge for a high school wide receiver, given his remarkable skills it was more than big enough.

With his lightning speed, sure hands, and shifty, elusive moves, DeSean became not just the best high school wide receiver in Southern California but one of the most highly touted players in the nation. During his senior year, he pulled down 60 passes for 1,075 yards. Of his 15 touchdowns that season, 8 were on plays of at least 60 yards—a good indication of just how explosive a player DeSean was. He led his Long Beach Polytechnic Jackrabbits team to a California Interscholastic Federation Southern Section football championship. In the title game, he starred in an unusual role. When the Jackrabbits' best cornerback got hurt on the opening kickoff, DeSean volunteered to take his place. Coach Raul Lara agreed, even though DeSean had never played defense and would have to cover one of the best high school wide receivers in Southern California. The move paid big dividends: DeSean grabbed two interceptions, returning one of them 68 yards for a touchdown as Poly beat Los Alamitos, 21–6.

The awards and honors piled up. DeSean received the 2004 Glenn Davis Award, which is given each year to the top high school player in Southern California. He was named California's Mr. Football State Player of the Year. *Parade Magazine* ranked him as an All-American.

General Richard A. Cody presents DeSean Jackson with the Pete Dawkins MVP Trophy after the U.S. Army All-American Bowl in San Antonio, Texas, January 15, 2005. DeSean caught seven passes for 141 yards as his West team won the game by a 35–3 score. The award capped off a great senior season for DeSean, during which his play attracted interest among coaches at the country's top college football programs.

Along with 79 other top high school players from around the country, DeSean received an invitation to participate in the 2005 U.S. Army All-American Bowl. In the game—held in San Antonio Texas, on January 15—he had seven receptions for 141 yards, and he also threw a touchdown pass on a trick play. DeSean would have scored a TD himself but for an ill-conceived bit of **showboating**. DeSean caught a pass at the 40-yard line, slipped a tackle, and raced down the sideline with no defender within five yards of him. About six yards from the end zone, however, DeSean leaped into the air and executed a forward flip. He landed about a half yard short of the goal line and fumbled. To add insult to injury, he was flagged for **unsportsmanlike conduct**. Coaches were outraged at the display, but DeSean wasn't concerned about that. After the game, he glibly told reporters:

> **"It was a mistake. I guess I should've taken off from the 5."**

Despite his premature touchdown celebration, DeSean was named the U.S. Army All-American Bowl's Most Valuable Player.

With his electrifying skills and his growing list of **gridiron** accomplishments, DeSean was aggressively recruited by many of the country's top college football programs. These schools included Florida, Florida State, Louisiana State University (LSU), Oklahoma, Tennessee, the University of California, and the University of Southern California (USC). Where would DeSean decide to go?

# A GOLDEN BEAR

By January 2005, DeSean Jackson had narrowed his college decision to two schools: California and USC. The universities are both in the Pacific-10 Conference. Pac-10 schools have a reputation not only for being fine academic institutions but also for fielding outstanding sports teams. In football, Pac-10 members compete at the highest level.

USC, located in DeSean's hometown of Los Angeles, boasted a dominant football program. Under head coach Pete Carroll, the Trojans had finished the 2003 season ranked #1 in the AP Poll after compiling a 12–1 record. The following season, as DeSean was deciding where to go to college, USC posted an undefeated 13–0 record,

**CROSS-CURRENTS**

Turn to page 49 to learn mor about the Pac-10, an athleti conference whose member sch have combined to win more th 400 national championships in men's and women's sports.

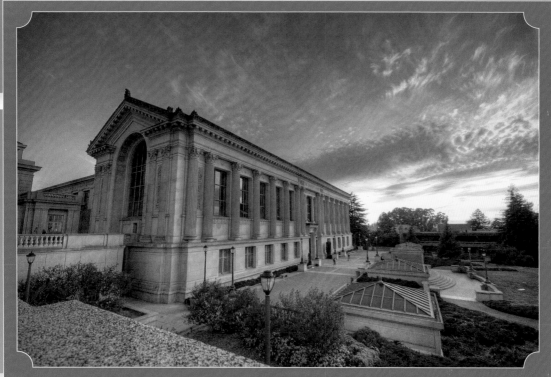

The University of California, Berkeley, was founded in 1868. Academically, it is ranked among the top universities in the world. This photo shows the Doe Memorial Library on the school's campus.

demolished Oklahoma in the Orange Bowl, and was the consensus national champion. If DeSean went to USC, he'd be joining a great team that would probably contend for another national title. He'd have the chance to play in top bowl games, where his talents might be showcased for a large national audience.

On the other hand, DeSean would be just one of many stars at USC. There was no guarantee he would get significant playing time—if he played at all—during his freshman season. At Cal, he'd have an opportunity to make an immediate impact. And while the Golden Bears weren't in USC's class, they were a very good team. Under Jeff Tedford, who took over as Cal's head coach in 2002, the Golden Bears had posted three straight winning seasons, including a 10–2 mark in 2004. They finished that season ranked ninth in the nation.

## Choosing the Bears

DeSean struggled with his decision. He saw advantages to both schools. On different occasions, DeSean would later admit, he told the head coaches of USC and Cal that he had chosen their school:

> **About a week after the Orange Bowl, I called up Coach Carroll and actually committed to him. I wanted to be a Trojan and felt like I would do great things there. The thing is though, I had also committed to Coach Tedford on an in-home visit earlier so I had two schools I loved and I really wasn't sure what I was going to do.**

As February approached—and with it the period when high school football stars sign letters of intent, committing them to a particular school—a host of media reports suggested that DeSean was going to choose USC. Many people were stunned when, during a Fox Sports show, DeSean theatrically pulled out a Cal hat and put it on his head. He explained:

> **About a week ago, I really started thinking hard about it and just felt like Cal was the best to help me reach my goals. Cal gives me an opportunity to come in and play right away and that was the most important thing to me. . . .**

> **I also think it's best for me to get away from home so I can grow up on my own. I love my family but I think I need to get away from them and gain some independence. I know I shocked a lot of people tonight because everyone thought I was going to 'SC. The thing with me though, I'm not a follower, I've never been that way. I had to do what was best for me and I didn't even tell my own family about this. I just kept it to myself so I could surprise everyone and I think I did.**

DeSean Jackson surprised some people when he decided to attend the University of California, Berkeley, on a football scholarship. At the school, DeSean gained the nickname "Tha-1," a reference to his uniform number and his position as the Golden Bears' most explosive receiver.

## Fantastic Freshman

In the late summer of 2005, DeSean traveled north to Berkeley to begin his collegiate career. He planned to major in social welfare.

DeSean celebrates after scoring a 31-yard touchdown on his first catch in a college football game, September 3, 2005. He scored another touchdown during the game as well, helping California rout Sacramento State by a 41–3 score.

On the football field, it didn't take DeSean long to show Golden Bears fans just how exciting a player he was. The first time he touched the ball, he scored. The 31-yard TD reception came in Cal's 2005 season opener, against Sacramento State. Later in that same game, DeSean took his first college punt return 49 yards for another touchdown.

DeSean turned in several other sensational performances during his freshman year. He scorched UCLA's defense for 128 yards on 10 catches, including a touchdown. Against New Mexico State he pulled down nine passes for 130 yards and a touchdown.

Despite DeSean's heroics, Cal struggled to an 8–4 record in 2005. The team did earn a bowl invitation, however. In the Las Vegas Bowl, DeSean helped the Golden Bears dispatch Brigham Young University, 35–28. He caught six passes for 130 yards and two touchdowns.

Brigham Young defender Kayle Buchanan can't stop DeSean from hauling in a touchdown pass from Cal quarterback Steve Levy during the third quarter of the Las Vegas Bowl, December 22, 2005. The score gave the Golden Bears a commanding 35-14 lead; they would go on to defeat the Cougars to finish the season with a 9-4 record.

DeSean finished the season as Cal's leading receiver. He'd tallied 38 receptions for 601 yards. He'd also notched seven touchdown receptions.

## Sophomore Sensation

If DeSean's freshman season had been outstanding, his sophomore season was even better. He caught 59 passes for an eye-popping 1,060 yards, or 18.0 yards per reception. He had nine touchdown receptions. He also returned four punts for touchdowns, setting a Pac-10 single-season record. DeSean's 2006 punt returns included a 72-yard scamper against UCLA, an 80-yarder against Arizona State, and a 95-yarder against Arizona. He led the entire nation in punt return average, with 18.2 yards per return.

Paced by DeSean's offensive fireworks, the Golden Bears had an excellent season. Their 7–2 conference record tied them with USC for the Pac-10 title. Cal's overall record was 10–3, and they obliterated Texas A&M in the Holiday Bowl, 45–10. In the final 2006 college football poll, Cal ranked 14th in the country.

For DeSean, the individual honors poured in. He was named first-team All Pac-10 as a receiver and a punt returner. As a punt returner, he was on the first-team All-America lists of the Associated Press, the *Sporting News*, and the Football Writers of America, among other organizations. Coach Jeff Tedford summed up the special qualities of his star wide receiver:

> **"He is gifted. No question his speed and feel for the game is as good as there is. He's so fast. He's the fastest player I've ever seen on the football field, and that puts him in a lot of positions to be successful. Any time you have DeSean, who can do the things he can, making people miss and hit things as fast as he does, it creates a huge advantage for you. With his explosive speed, you really have to take notice. If you leave him one-on-one, he's got the speed and quickness to really make plays."**

This 36-yard catch in a game against Oregon was one of nine touchdown receptions by DeSean Jackson during the 2006 season. In this game, DeSean also returned a punt 65 yards for a touchdown, helping the Golden Bears beat the Ducks, 45–24.

## Disappointing Season

In his junior year, DeSean Jackson picked up where he had left off in his sophomore season. With the score tied, 14–14, in Cal's 2007 season opener against Tennessee, DeSean fielded a punt near the left sideline. He slipped the first tackler, then danced to the right, looking for an opening. Tennessee linebacker Adam Myers-White had a perfect angle and appeared certain to make the tackle. Just before Myers-White hit him, however, DeSean jumped backward, leaving the Tennessee linebacker grasping at air. An instant later, DeSean had accelerated to full speed. He rounded the corner and raced 77 yards for a touchdown. An announcer noted that DeSean's astonishing move was the kind of play usually confined to video games. Cal went on to defeat Tennessee, 45–31.

DeSean showed yet another dimension to his game in the Golden Bears' second contest, against Colorado State. He took the handoff on an end-around play and ran 73 yards for a touchdown. It was the only rushing TD of his college career, and it helped Cal get the win, 34–28.

The Golden Bears, ranked 12th in the country at the start of the season, notched three more victories in a row. The 5–0 start catapulted Cal to a #2 ranking.

Then everything began to go wrong. Cal lost six of its next seven games before defeating Air Force in the Armed Forces Bowl. The Golden Bears finished with a 7–6 overall record and a dismal 3–6 conference mark.

During his team's swoon, DeSean had been vocal about what he thought needed to be done. He told reporters that Coach Tedford should call more pass plays, especially on first and second down. This echoed opinions DeSean had earlier shared with the media:

CROSS-CURRENTS

In 2002, Jeff Tedford became the University of California's 32nd head football coach. For a brief profile of the man who coached DeSean Jackson in college, turn to page 50.

**"I think Coach Tedford just has to let us play loose. Let us off the chain. We're like pit bulls strapped down. I know he's a great coach, but he could just let us do some simple things. . . . Everything ain't gotta be hard."**

Publicly, Tedford brushed aside the criticism from his star receiver. But when asked whether DeSean was a team leader, the coach refused to comment. DeSean had been benched in the first quarter of the Armed Forces Bowl for an unspecified violation of team rules. There appeared to be considerable tension in the Cal locker room.

Most college wide receivers would be satisfied with the kind of season DeSean posted in 2007: 65 receptions, 762 yards, six touchdowns. But in yards per catch, total yards, and touchdowns, DeSean's production was way down from 2006. In addition, the only punt he returned for a TD had come in the season opener.

Injuries were part of the reason for the decline in DeSean's productivity. Throughout much of the season, he had been hampered by a sore finger and a strained thigh muscle. But the fact that he hadn't been 100 percent didn't make the 2007 season any easier for DeSean to accept. He noted:

> **"I definitely think my junior year was a disappointment and one of the toughest years I had at college, but I learned a lot. At times, I got a little frustrated, but it taught me to be patient and make the most of my opportunities."**

On January 15, 2008, DeSean Jackson announced that he would not be returning to Cal for his senior year. The 21-year-old had decided to enter the NFL draft.

California head coach Jeff Tedford congratulates DeSean Jackson after a touchdown catch. Although Tedford appreciated the speed and talent of his star wide receiver, there were tensions between coach and player after DeSean publicly criticized Tedford during a 2007 losing streak.

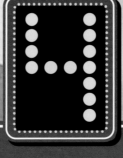

# FLYING WITH THE EAGLES

O n April 26, NFL coaches, general managers, and scouts descended on New York City for the 2008 college draft. Opinions varied about when DeSean Jackson would be picked. Some experts believed his blazing speed and dazzling punt return skills would make him a first-round selection. Others believed he was too small for the NFL. One NFC scouting director said:

> **"He's slight of build, and that will be his issue. He's a peanut. We would discount him because of his size."**

Others doubted DeSean's work ethic. Through intense weight training, football players typically get bigger during their college years. Yet DeSean had entered and left Cal at virtually the same weight. Did that mean he had been slacking off in the weight room?

**CROSS-CURRENTS**

*In a 20-year NFL career, Jerry Rice set records in numerous receiving catego-ries. For a profile of the San Francisco 49ers legend, see page 51.*

One person who championed DeSean was Jerry Rice. Rice, the all-time NFL leader in touchdown receptions, had been sharing his knowledge and experience with DeSean since the young man decided to enter the NFL draft. Of his **protégé**, Rice declared:

**❝He has all the talent in the world. There's no reason he can't be everything he wants to be at the next level.❞**

Surrounded by family members and friends, DeSean Jackson (center) learns that he has been selected by the Philadelphia Eagles in the second round of the 2008 NFL draft. DeSean was the 49th player drafted that year.

In the end, however, the doubters prevailed. DeSean slipped to the second round. The Philadelphia Eagles were the beneficiary. The Eagles signed DeSean to a four-year contract worth just over $3 million. DeSean would have made considerably more had he been selected in the first round.

After a good preseason, DeSean became the first rookie that Andy Reid had ever started on opening day in his 10 years as the Eagles' head coach. DeSean rewarded Reid's confidence with his six-pass, 106-yard performance against the Rams.

## Blunder in Dallas

Philadelphia's second game of the 2008 season was a huge one. The Eagles were on the road, facing NFC East rivals the Dallas Cowboys.

Fans who stayed up to watch the *Monday Night Football* telecast were treated to an entertaining, back-and-forth, high-scoring game. Ultimately, the Cowboys came from behind in the fourth quarter to eke out a 41–37 victory.

DeSean put up some impressive numbers in his introduction to a national pro-football audience. He gained 110 yards on six receptions. Unfortunately, the only play of DeSean's that fans would remember was a major blunder. With just under eight minutes left in the second quarter, the Eagles faced third and 10 from their own 40-yard line. Dallas was holding a slim 21–20 lead. Donovan McNabb dropped back to pass, and DeSean found a seam in the defense. He blew past the cornerback and safety. McNabb uncorked a perfect pass, which DeSean hauled in at the Dallas 10-yard line. He strode unimpeded toward the end zone, celebrating his first NFL touchdown by flipping the ball behind his back. There was just one problem: DeSean hadn't quite crossed the goal line when he flipped the ball away. After the officials reviewed the play, they decided that it wasn't a touchdown but rather a fumble. As had happened four years earlier at the U.S. Army All-American Bowl, DeSean's premature celebration had cost him a touchdown. Fortunately for DeSean, the Eagles retained the ball, and on the next play Brian Westbrook plunged into the end zone on a one-yard run.

After the game, DeSean chalked up his mental lapse to youth and inexperience. He told reporters:

Costly miscalculation: DeSean Jackson drops the ball before going into the end zone during a Monday night game against Dallas, September 15, 2008. It would have been the rookie's first NFL touchdown. Fortunately for DeSean, his premature celebration did not cost the team any points, as the Eagles kept possession and scored on the next play.

**"I thought I was in the end zone. You know, sometimes things happen like that, and I'm still young. I still have to learn. It definitely won't happen again, though."**

**CROSS-CURRENTS**

Philadelphians have a reputation for taking their sports very seriously, and this is especially true of the Eagles' faithful. For details, turn to page 53.

Many fans weren't ready to dismiss the incident so quickly, however. DeSean was widely ridiculed for his gaffe. He was called an idiot, a bonehead, and the victim of a brain cramp, among other things. In Philadelphia, some talk-radio callers screeched that Andy Reid should bench DeSean. As is his custom, Reid said little in public about the matter, and he didn't heed the calls that DeSean be benched. McNabb defended his rookie wideout, praising DeSean's work ethic and his mental preparation for games.

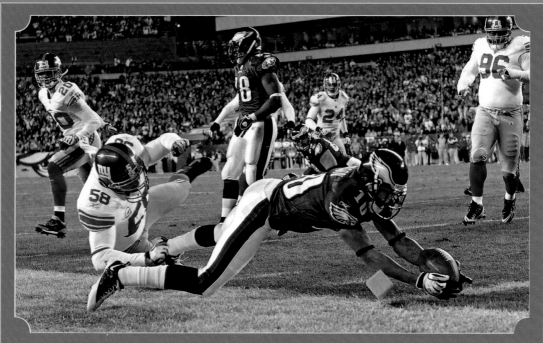

DeSean dives into the end zone to score his first NFL rushing touchdown, on a nine-yard run against the New York Giants, November 9, 2008. He also caught four passes for 61 yards during the game.

## Ups and Downs

DeSean recorded his first NFL touchdown in week 4, in a game against the Chicago Bears. He scored on a 22-yard pass from McNabb. Unfortunately, Chicago spoiled the day, beating the Birds by a score of 24–20.

The following week, DeSean notched his first TD on a punt return. Against the Washington Redskins, he took a first-quarter kick 68 yards to the end zone. Again, however, his efforts came in a losing cause, as Washington dealt the Eagles a 23–17 defeat.

After the loss to the Redskins, Philadelphia got back on track, winning its next three games. DeSean contributed with a six-catch, 98-yard performance against the San Francisco 49ers, and a three-catch, 72-yard outing against the Atlanta Falcons. At the halfway mark of the season, the Birds' record stood at 5–3.

On November 9, Lincoln Financial Field was rocking when the Eagles hosted the defending Super Bowl champion New York Giants. To the delight of the hometown crowd, DeSean opened the scoring with a nine-yard touchdown run in the first quarter. It was his first rushing

TD in the NFL. Unfortunately, that milestone would come in a losing cause, as the Giants left town with a hard-fought 36–31 victory.

The following week, the Eagles traveled to Cincinnati to take on the lowly Bengals, who had just one win against eight losses for the season. The afternoon would turn into a long exercise in frustration for the visitors, who had all kinds of trouble getting the ball into the end zone. At the end of the fourth quarter, the score was tied at 13 points apiece. Neither team managed to score in the overtime period, so the Eagles limped out of Cincinnati with a pathetic tie.

The next week, the Eagles traveled to Baltimore to face the Ravens. It wasn't much of a contest. Philadelphia managed just one touchdown, absorbing a 36–7 beating at the hands of Baltimore.

The Eagles' record now stood at 5–5–1. Their playoff hopes for 2008 seemed dead.

## Playoff Run

On November 28, paced by Donovan McNabb, Brian Westbrook, and DeSean Jackson, the Eagles thrashed the Arizona Cardinals, 48–20. DeSean grabbed six passes for 76 yards and a touchdown.

The following week, despite the fact that DeSean was held without a single catch, the Eagles beat the New York Giants. The final score was 20–14.

Next up for the Birds was a Monday night game against the Cleveland Browns. DeSean contributed five receptions for 77 yards in a 30–10 Eagles victory.

The three straight wins boosted Philadelphia's record to 8–5–1. Again there appeared to be a glimmer of hope for a playoff berth. But the Eagles came out flat in their next game, losing 10–3 to the Washington Redskins.

To get into the postseason now, Philadelphia would need a lot of help from other teams in the last week of the regular season. One thing that had to happen was for the sad-sack Oakland Raiders, who carried a 4–11 record and had long since been eliminated from playoff contention, to beat the 9–6 Tampa Bay Buccaneers, who were competing for a playoff spot. Incredibly, Oakland did just that. Buoyed, the Eagles trounced Dallas, 44–6. They finished with a record of 9–6–1, good enough to secure an NFC **wild card** spot.

## A Lot on His Mind

For DeSean Jackson, this should have been an exciting time. In his first year in the NFL, he would be playing in the postseason.

Only days before the Eagles' wild card matchup against the Minnesota Vikings, however, DeSean got some troubling news from California. His father had taken ill. Bill Jackson was diagnosed with pancreatic cancer. DeSean tried to focus on the upcoming game, but it was difficult.

The Vikings held DeSean in check in the wild card game, which was played in Minnesota on January 4, 2009. He caught just one pass, for 24 yards. Nevertheless, the Eagles won the game, 26–14, to advance to the divisional playoff round.

On January 11, the Eagles traveled to the unfriendly confines of Giants Stadium in East Rutherford, New Jersey. They entered the divisional playoff game as big underdogs. But they weren't intimidated by the defending Super Bowl champs. Philadelphia's defense stifled the Giants, and—with DeSean leading all receivers with 81 yards on four catches—the Birds' offense drove for two touchdowns and added three field goals. Final score: Eagles, 23; Giants, 11.

**CROSS-CURRENTS**

*Fewer than 5 percent of people with pancreatic cancer survive five years after the diagnosis. To learn more about this deadly disease see page 54.*

For the Eagles, all that stood in the way of a trip to Super Bowl XLIII was the Arizona Cardinals, a team Philadelphia had manhandled in week 13. The NFC championship game would be played in Phoenix on January 18.

Five and a half minutes into the game, the Cardinals jumped out to a 7–0 lead. In the second quarter, they poured it on. At halftime Philadelphia trailed by a score of 24–6. For most of the third quarter, the Eagles could get nothing going offensively. Then, with 4:08 left in the quarter, Donovan McNabb connected with tight end Brent Celek for a touchdown. The Eagles got the ball back quickly and, with just 49 seconds remaining in the quarter, McNabb and Celek hooked up for another TD. With a quarter left to play, the Eagles had suddenly pulled within five points.

It wouldn't take long for Philadelphia to strike again. With only four minutes gone in the fourth quarter, the Eagles had the ball at their own 38-yard line. McNabb rolled to his right and heaved a bomb to DeSean Jackson, who was streaking downfield a half step ahead of Cardinals cornerback Dominique Rodgers-Cromartie. As the ball came down, Rodgers-Cromartie leaped up and tipped it. But the deflection didn't break DeSean's concentration. He juggled the ball, then pulled it in and scooted into the end zone. The hometown crowd was stunned. After a failed two-point conversion attempt, the Eagles led, 25–24.

Perhaps the biggest catch of DeSean Jackson's rookie season came in the NFC championship game on January 18, 2009. With 10:45 left in the game, DeSean beat Arizona Cardinals cornerback Dominique Rodgers-Cromartie for a 62-yard touchdown. The score gave the Eagles a 25–24 lead, but they couldn't hold on. Arizona pulled out a 32–25 victory to advance to the Super Bowl.

Arizona fought back. With just 2:53 remaining on the game clock, Cardinals quarterback Kurt Warner tossed a short TD pass, then connected on a two-point conversion, to put his team ahead by a score of 32–25. Philadelphia was unable to rally, and Arizona became the NFC champion.

## An Outstanding Season

Although the season had ended on a disappointing note, DeSean Jackson could look back on his rookie year with a sense of accomplishment. He led the team, and established Eagles rookie records, in both receptions (62) and receiving yards (912). He also led the team in yards per reception (14.7).

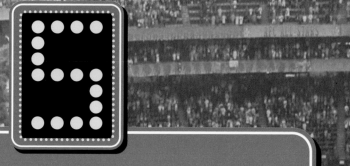

# DEDICATED TO A DAD

In the off-season, DeSean brought his father from Long Beach to Philadelphia. Sadly, Bill Jackson's pancreatic cancer was incurable. He died at the Hospital of the University of Pennsylvania on May 14, 2009. A few weeks later, as he and his Eagles teammates gathered for **minicamp**, DeSean spoke about his loss:

> **"**Everything about me in sports is credited to him. Without him I wouldn't be here. It was a blessing to have a father who did everything like that for me. We had a great relationship. He never accepted anything but the best from me.

After returning a punt for a touchdown in the first game of the 2009 season, DeSean Jackson celebrates in the end zone. Before the season, the star wide receiver had vowed to play hard in memory of his father, who had died from cancer in May 2009.

**"I'm going to be just as strong as my dad would have wanted me to be. He wouldn't have wanted me to sit around and mope, tuck my head under my tail. . . . It's one day at a time. I'm just trying to stay strong for my family. This is a hard period for me. But I'm hanging in there."**

DeSean recognized that, more than any other person, his father had shaped who he had become. His father had put him on a path to success—in football and in life. In gratitude for that, DeSean said:

**"This whole season, the rest of my career, I'm dedicating to my dad."**

## Most Explosive Player in the NFL

DeSean's 2009 season was the kind of which Bill Jackson would have been proud. In game after game, DeSean reeled off huge plays, staking his claim to the title of most explosive player in the NFL.

DeSean's offensive fireworks began in the Eagles' season opener, against the Carolina Panthers. In the second quarter of the game, DeSean took a punt return 85 yards for a touchdown. The Eagles won the game, 38–10, but the victory proved costly: quarterback Donovan McNabb suffered cracked ribs.

With backup QB Kevin Kolb in the lineup in week 2, the Eagles faced a tough New Orleans Saints team. DeSean had 101 receiving yards on four receptions, including a 71-yard TD catch. But Philadelphia was no match for the Saints, falling by a score of 48–22.

DeSean helped his team get back on track in week 3. Against the Kansas City Chiefs, he scored another long touchdown—this one on a 64-yard reception. By game's end, the Eagles owned a 34–14 win, and DeSean had logged 149 yards on six catches.

After a bye week, the Eagles returned to action against the Tampa Bay Buccaneers, a game that also saw the return of Donovan McNabb. DeSean was not a factor, catching just one short pass, but McNabb found other targets to pace the Birds to victory.

DeSean returned to form the following week, catching six passes for 94 yards. But his Eagles suffered an embarrassing 13–9 loss to the Oakland Raiders, one of the league's weakest teams. Philadelphia appeared to be foundering. Someone needed to step forward to right the ship.

That someone turned out to be DeSean Jackson. On October 26, in a *Monday Night Football* matchup against the Washington Redskins, DeSean powered his team to victory with some huge plays. On the fourth play from scrimmage, DeSean took the ball on a reverse and raced down the left sideline for a 67-yard touchdown. It was the longest Eagles run of the season. In the second quarter, DeSean scored again on another big play—a 57-yard pass from McNabb. *Monday Night Football* analyst Jon Gruden, a former NFL head coach, gushed that DeSean was piling up "more explosive plays than anybody in NFL history." After the Eagles had sealed a 27–17 win, Redskins coach Jim Zorn shook his head and said simply, "He's wicked fast." DeSean's heroics in Washington earned him NFL Offensive Player of the Week honors.

Showing his spectacular speed, DeSean breaks away from Kansas City defenders to score a touchdown, September 27, 2009.

The following Sunday, DeSean was at it again, demonstrating how "wicked fast" he is. The occasion was a home game against the New York Giants. DeSean sliced through the Giants' defense for a second-quarter touchdown reception covering 54 yards. The Eagles spanked the G-men, 40–17, to boost their record to 5–2. The team seemed to be clicking.

On November 8, however, Philadelphia would face a tough test when the Dallas Cowboys—who also boasted a 5–2 record—came to town. The game was close throughout. But in the fourth quarter it was the Cowboys' star young receiver, Miles Austin, who came up with the big play. Austin grabbed a 49-yard Tony Romo pass to put Dallas ahead for good.

The Eagles suffered another loss, against the San Diego Chargers, the following week. DeSean had a good game, catching eight passes for 91 yards. But that was not enough to prevent the surging Chargers

In a *Monday Night Football* game against the Washington Redskins, DeSean Jackson showed the prime-time audience why he is one of the most explosive young players in the NFL today. He caught two passes, including a 57-yard touchdown, and ran 67 yards for another score.

from recording a 31–23 win. The Eagles' record dropped to 5–4, and again their season appeared to be teetering on the brink of collapse.

As he'd done before, DeSean Jackson responded with an explosive performance. On November 22, with the Eagles visiting Chicago's Soldier Field, he grabbed eight passes for 107 yards. His 48-yard touchdown strike from McNabb helped Philadelphia escape the Windy City with a 24–20 win.

DeSean had now recorded seven touchdowns during the 2009 season. All had gone for more than 45 yards. The Eagles' second-year wide receiver had truly emerged as one of the NFL's most exciting players. He was a genuine game-changer.

## Hard Knock

DeSean caught another touchdown pass on November 29, in the season's second Eagles-Redskins matchup. DeSean's eighth TD of 2009, a first-quarter hookup with Donovan McNabb, went for "only" 35 yards. It was the first time all season DeSean had scored from less than 45 yards out.

What happened in the third quarter, however, was far more significant. DeSean grabbed a six-yard pass over the middle and was hit hard by Redskins linebacker London Fletcher and cornerback Justin Tryon. DeSean crumbled to the turf. He remained on the ground only for a few seconds before getting up and walking to the sideline. But he didn't return to the game.

In his postgame press conference, Coach Andy Reid revealed that DeSean had suffered a concussion but that it didn't appear too serious:

**"He was just a little groggy, but he was able to get up and get off the field and all that fairly quick."**

In the past, concussions rarely sidelined NFL players for very long. It was generally expected that a player who sustained a concussion would be back in the lineup for the next game. In fact, players sometimes sat out only a few plays, returning to the field a few *minutes* after a concussion. "Getting your bell rung" wasn't believed to present any special danger.

Today, that belief is known to be incorrect. A growing body of evidence shows that suffering one concussion can make a player more susceptible to further concussions—especially if the player returns to action before his brain has fully recovered from the first trauma—and that multiple concussions can lead to serious and permanent damage to the brain.

Thus, because DeSean Jackson had some lingering headaches in the days after his concussion against Washington, the Eagles decided to keep him out of the lineup in their next game. When they faced the Falcons on December 6, it would be without their leading receiver.

**CROSS-CURRENTS**

Concussions are fairly common in contact sports such as football. To find out what causes them and why they should always be taken seriously, turn to page 54.

Eagles teammates Brent Celek (87), Donovan McNabb (5), and Jamaal Jackson (67) stand by DeSean Jackson, who lies on the field after a hard third-quarter hit during the November 29, 2009, game against the Redskins. DeSean suffered a concussion, and sat out the rest of the game, as well as the next week's game.

Despite DeSean's absence, Philadelphia managed to win. The Eagles dispatched Atlanta, 34–7, to improve their record to 8–4.

## Giant Killer

DeSean returned to the lineup on December 13, as Philadelphia traveled up the New Jersey Turnpike to face the 7–5 New York Giants in a Sunday night showdown. The game had playoff implications for both teams.

The Eagles drew first blood, scoring a touchdown on their initial possession. The TD—which came on a seven-yard toss from Donovan McNabb to Brent Celek—was set up by DeSean Jackson's 32-yard catch of a Michael Vick pass.

Running back Brandon Jacobs coughed up the ball on the Giants' first possession, and Eagles cornerback Sheldon Brown returned the fumble 60 yards for a touchdown. The G-men appeared in danger of getting blown out.

But the Giants regained their poise, battling back with a field goal and a touchdown to draw within four points of the visitors early in the second quarter. An Eagles field goal made the score 17–10.

With under five minutes left in the first half, Giants punter Jeff Feagles booted the ball from the New York 31-yard line. The 41-yard punt was well placed: When DeSean Jackson fielded the ball at the Eagles' 28-yard line, he was pinned near the left sideline, apparently having little room to run. DeSean took a few quick steps to the right, then danced backward as the Giants' defenders closed in. He darted left toward the sideline and turned upfield, leaving his pursuers a step behind. Eagles blocks rubbed out two would-be tacklers, and DeSean was off to the races. At the New York 45-yard line, Feagles made a vain attempt to force DeSean out of bounds, but the punter ended up grasping air. DeSean strode down the sideline and into the end zone. The 72-yard return put Philadelphia up by a score of 24–10. It also established an Eagles franchise record, for most career touchdowns on punt returns (three).

The Birds took a 30–17 cushion into the locker room at halftime, but New York refused to go away quietly. The G-men scored a pair of third-quarter touchdowns to grab their first lead of the game, 31–30.

After the ensuing kickoff, Donovan McNabb dialed up DeSean Jackson on the first play from scrimmage. DeSean burned the Giants' secondary for a 60-yard touchdown catch that put the Birds up for good. They went on to win the NFC East shoot-out by a score of 45–38.

DeSean finished the game with monster stats: six receptions for 178 yards. Moreover, by virtue of his two long TDs, he tied the NFL single-season record for most touchdowns of 50 yards or longer, at eight. Elroy "Crazy Legs" Hirsch of the Los Angeles Rams had first accomplished that feat in 1951, and Devin Hester of the Chicago Bears had matched it in 2007.

Osi Umenyiora, the Giants All-Pro defensive end, acknowledged the obvious—that DeSean had simply killed his team. Umenyiora said:

**"He got us, man. We had a plan but . . . we just couldn't cover him."**

In his postgame remarks, Andy Reid emphasized DeSean's enthusiasm and his confidence. The coach said:

**"He loves playing. When the games are on the line, he wants the ball and we'll give it to him."**

## Eagles Grounded

After defeating the Giants, the Birds had a 9–4 record and were perched atop the NFC East. If they won their remaining three games, they would be guaranteed to host at least one playoff game at Lincoln Financial Field.

Philadelphia moved toward that goal by spanking the San Francisco 49ers, 27–13, at the Linc in week 15. DeSean turned in another huge performance, pulling down six catches for 140 yards and a touchdown.

The following week, DeSean helped his team turn back a plucky Denver Broncos squad with a first-quarter touchdown reception. It was his ninth TD catch of the season.

In the final week of the regular season, the Eagles traveled to Texas to do battle with the Dallas Cowboys. Much was at stake. If they won, the Birds would secure the second seed in the NFC, giving them a first-round playoff bye and home-field advantage at least until the NFC championship game. But the 'Boys dominated Philadelphia, neutralizing the Eagles' offense en route to a 24–0 whitewashing. DeSean was held to just three catches for 47 yards, and he dropped a couple balls he should have caught.

Nevertheless, DeSean rejected the suggestion, made by Dallas reporters, that the Cowboys had his number. "What makes you think I got shut down?" he asked.

"The best players in the N.F.L. have great games, and you're going to have games that are not great games. You have to accept that, being a special player in the N.F.L. It's not going to break me or make me. I'm still going to go out there and do everything I can to help my team win and be successful."

The Cowboys' week 17 victory set up a rematch, again at Texas Stadium, in the wild card round of the playoffs. Despite the drubbing his team had received in the regular-season finale, DeSean was confident about the Eagles' chances in the wild card game. On his Twitter feed, he promised that the Birds would "sting" Dallas on January 9.

That didn't happen. Again Dallas dominated, pushing the Eagles around on both sides of the ball. DeSean was once more held in check. He caught just three passes for 14 yards. While he did reach the end zone on a four-yard pass from Donovan McNabb, that score came in the fourth quarter, after the outcome of the game had been decided. The Eagles' season ended with a 34–14 beating.

After the game, a humbled DeSean told reporters:

"It's embarrassing. We never planned to lose like this."

## Action Jackson

Despite the abrupt end to the Eagles' season, DeSean Jackson had truly come into his own. He finished his second year in the NFL with 63 receptions for 1,167 yards and nine touchdowns. His 18.5 yards-per-catch average, highest in the league, demonstrated just how dangerous a receiver #10 had become. DeSean was also the NFL's best punt returner in 2009, averaging 15.2 yards per return and notching two touchdowns.

Fellow players, coaches, and fans recognized DeSean's ascent into the ranks of the NFL's elite players by voting him into the Pro Bowl. DeSean made the NFC roster at two positions, wide receiver and kick returner. According to the NFL, it was the first time a player had been a Pro Bowl starter at both those positions in the same year.

Given his exquisite skills and his passion for the game, it seems likely that DeSean Jackson will achieve other firsts before his NFL career is done.

**CROSS-CURRENTS**

The Pro Bowl is the NFL's annual all-star game. Turn to page 55 to learn more about the game.

# Donovan McNabb

Philadelphia Eagles quarterback Donovan McNabb was born in Chicago in 1976 and went to Syracuse University. The Eagles made him the second player chosen in the 1999 NFL draft. McNabb has played in Philadelphia ever since.

Fans, players, and coaches voted McNabb into the Pro Bowl every year from 2000 through 2004. During those years, the team went to four NFC championship games. After finally winning the championship after the 2004 season, the Eagles reached Super Bowl XXXIX.

McNabb's best season was 2004, the season the Eagles went to the Super Bowl. This was the first year that he had wide receiver Terrell Owens available to catch his passes. During the regular season, McNabb completed 64 percent of his passes, threw 31 touchdowns, and ran for three other scores. His 104.7 passer rating—a statistic designed to measure a quarterback's efficiency—ranked fourth among NFL QBs. McNabb set the NFL record for most consecutive completed passes, throwing 24 over the course of two games. He became the first quarterback in league history to throw more than 30 touchdown passes and fewer than 10 interceptions in a season. (He was picked just eight times during the regular season.) (Go back to page 7.) ◀◀

*Eagles quarterback Donovan McNabb (5) directs the offense during a 2009 playoff game against the Minnesota Vikings.*

# The NFL Draft

Each year the NFL conducts what is officially termed a *player selection meeting*, commonly called the draft. This is the process by which the NFL brings new players from the ranks of college football into the league.

The draft is organized into a series of seven rounds. In each round, each of the 32 NFL teams gets to pick a player. The order in which teams pick is determined by their success the previous year. The team with the worst record gets the first choice. The team with the second-worst record gets the second choice, and so on. The Super Bowl winner gets the last pick of the round. The draft is organized this way to try to balance the talent levels among the teams. Teams can change the order of their pick, however, if they trade a player. The Super Bowl winner, for example, could trade a star player for a higher pick.

The draft takes place near the end of April, and it is a huge media event. The top players usually attend and dress well for the event. Fans often boo or cheer a particular pick.

For NFL coaches and team executives, however, the hype is beside the point. Their focus is on getting the players who will most be able to help their team win. A good draft can greatly improve a team's performance—and in some cases, the improvement is immediate. On the other hand, several bad picks can hamper a club's chances for years to come.

## Diamonds in the Rough

In the early years of the NFL, teams often did not know much about the players they drafted. They depended on word of mouth or phone calls to sportswriters or college coaches.

That is no longer the case. Scouting has become a science. Enormous files are maintained on prospects. Would-be draftees are weighed, measured, timed, and even given intelligence and psychological tests.

Most of the time, this homework pays off. A recent study of All-Pro players over the last five years showed that half were drafted in the first round.

Sometimes, however, players have slipped through the cracks. In the 2002 draft, for example, 90 players were selected before the Eagles finally chose Brian Westbrook in the third round. Westbrook became one of the most versatile running backs in the NFL. Occasionally, a player is completely overlooked on draft day, only to go onto have a Hall of Fame NFL career. Undrafted Hall of Famers include quarterback Warren Moon, and defensive backs Willie Brown and Dick "Night Train" Lane. (Go back to page 7.) ◀◀

# Jackrabbit Pride

With an enrollment of about 5,000 students, Long Beach Polytechnic is the second-largest public high school in California. Polytechnic—or Poly, as it is often called—draws students not only from Long Beach but also from portions of the adjoining city of Lakewood and from Signal Hill, a small city that is surrounded by Long Beach.

Established in 1895, Poly boasts a long tradition of athletic success. In fact, in 2005 *Sports Illustrated* named it the "Sports School of the Century." That honor recognized the dominance of Long Beach Polytechnic Jackrabbits teams in sports ranging from cross-country and track to football, baseball, basketball, and badminton. Poly has fielded many regional and state champions in boys' and girls' sports.

A host of professional athletes honed their skills as members of Jackrabbits teams. Tennis superstar Billie Jean King, winner of 12 Grand Slam titles, was a standout at Poly. Among the half dozen former Jackrabbits to play major league baseball are Hall of Fame member Tony Gwynn, who won eight National League batting titles during a 20-year career with the San Diego Padres; and Chase Utley of the Philadelphia Phillies, considered by many to be the best second baseman in the game today.

*Long Beach Poly graduate Willie McGinest won three Super Bowls with the New England Patriots during his 15-year NFL career.*

In no sport, however, have more Poly alumni gone on to the professional ranks than in football. Since the school's founding, more than 50 former Jackrabbits have played in the NFL. At least 16 have been drafted since 1988.

What explains this extraordinary record? "The main thing you have to remember is that tradition never hurts," Poly football head coach Raul Lara told *USA Today* in 2008, after the Jackrabbits had won their 17th California Interscholastic Federation Southern Section championship. Making the Jackrabbits squad is the dream of young football players throughout the Long Beach area. Competition is fierce, and even the most naturally gifted athletes are driven to excel. (Go back to page 15.) ◀◀

# The Pac-10

The Pacific-10 Conference is made up of universities from four western states. They are: the University of Arizona; Arizona State University; the University of California, Berkeley (Cal); the University of California, Los Angeles (UCLA); the University of Southern California (USC); Stanford University; Oregon State University; the University of Oregon; the University of Washington; and Washington State University.

The Pac-10 traces its history to 1915, when the Pacific Coast Conference was founded. Its charter members were Cal, Oregon, Oregon State, and Washington. In the years that followed, the conference expanded to include other schools. It also changed names several times.

In 1978 the Pac-10 took its current name with the addition of Arizona and Arizona State to the Pacific-8 Conference. Since then, the conference has maintained the same membership.

Over the years, the schools of the Pac-10 have enjoyed enormous athletic success. As of the 2008–09 season, the 10 schools had won a combined 412 National Collegiate Athletic Association (NCAA) team titles, in men's and women's sports. UCLA led the way with 104 championships. The Bruins were followed by Stanford, with 97 titles, and USC, with 88. (Go back to page 18.) ◀◀

*A marching band performs at halftime of a Pac-10 football game between California and the University of Oregon.*

# Jeff Tedford

When Jeff Tedford took over as head coach at Cal in 2002, the university's football program was in shambles. Tom Holmoe, who preceded Tedford as head coach of the Golden Bears, had stumbled to a record of 12–43 during his five-year tenure. Cal's 1–10 season in 2001 prompted Holmoe's resignation, but the team had also been rocked two years earlier by a scandal involving ineligible players. Tedford quickly turned Cal's program around. He steered the team to a 7–5 record in 2002. Through 2009, his teams had compiled eight consecutive winning seasons and appeared in seven postseason bowl games.

Tedford was born in Lynwood, California, in 1961. He played quarterback in high school and junior college before starring at Fresno State, where he set several school passing records.

After graduating from Fresno in 1983, he played for a half dozen seasons in the Canadian Football League. He was later hired as a quarterbacks coach at Fresno. He became the offensive coordinator there before leaving in 1998 to accept the offensive coordinator job at Oregon. His first head coaching opportunity came when Cal called.

(Go back to page 26.)◀◀

*Since taking over as head coach at the University of California, Berkeley, in 2002, Jeff Tedford has never had a losing season. From 2005 to 2007, when DeSean Jackson was on the team, the Golden Bears won 25 games and lost 13.*

# Jerry Rice

While DeSean Jackson was in high school and college, he idolized wide receiver Jerry Rice, who set many NFL records during a career that began with the San Francisco 49ers in 1985 and ended with the Seattle Seahawks in 2004.

Born in Mississippi in 1962, Rice grew up to play college football at Mississippi Valley State University. His football coach there, Archie Cooley, described Rice as a hard worker to *USA Today* in 2003:

> **"Jerry was a workaholic, a kid who couldn't get enough of football. At Mississippi Valley, Jerry showed so much leadership. He showed other receivers they had to play catch before and after practice. He was always the one in front when they ran sprints and the bleachers."**

While Rice was in college, San Francisco 49ers coach Bill Walsh came to watch him play. Cooley told *USA Today* about that visit:

> **"We're playing a game in Houston on a Saturday and the 49ers were playing the Oilers that Sunday and Bill Walsh comes to our practice and says, 'Coach Cooley, which one is Jerry Rice? I'd like to watch him.' After practice, Bill tells me, 'I want that kid, and I'll do whatever it takes to get him.'"**

The 49ers, for which Rice played the bulk of his career, picked Rice during the first round of the 1985 draft. But his first year did not go smoothly. In 2003 Rice told the *New York Times* he had "balls dropped all over the place," and it took him a while to adjust to being part of the 49ers and professional football:

> **"I was very embarrassed because I knew I could catch the football and I just had to put my finger on what was a distraction for me. And once I did that, I let my natural ability take over."**

That ability led Rice to set numerous NFL records. They include: most career pass receptions (1,549); most consecutive games during which he caught passes (274); most career yards gained (22,895); most seasons in which he gained 1,000 or more yards in pass receptions (14); most yards gained in a season (1,848); most career touchdowns (197); most touchdowns in a season (22); and most consecutive games scoring at least one touchdown (13). In addition, Rice is in a three-way tie for most touchdowns scored in a game, with five.

Rice played in four Super Bowls. In Super Bowl XXIII, when San Francisco beat Denver, Rice was the game's most valuable player. (Go back to page 29.) ◀◀

# Philly: A Football Kind of Town

Philadelphia sports fans are renowned—some would say notorious—for the intensity of their passion. Opposing teams playing in the City of Brotherly Love can expect to be serenaded by a chorus of boos, along with all manner of jeers and personal insults. Underperforming Philadelphia athletes aren't spared the wrath of their fans, either. Some of the raw emotion stems from repeated disappointment: Philadelphia's four major pro teams—baseball's Phillies, basketball's 76ers, hockey's Flyers, and football's Eagles—have won just one championship in the past 25 years.

For loyalty, enthusiasm, and occasional misbehavior, the Eagles' faithful take a backseat to none of their Philly-sports-fan peers, or to the fans of other NFL teams. Some of their antics have passed into legend. In December 1968, fans pelted a man dressed as Santa Claus with snowballs. In 1989 snowballs—along with batteries and beer—rained down on the hated Dallas Cowboys and their coach, Jimmy Johnson. During a Monday night game against the San Francisco 49ers in 1997, controversial calls by the officials and the poor play of the Eagles fueled a series of fights in the stands, and one fan even fired a flare gun over the field. That debacle prompted the team and the city of Philadelphia to establish a courtroom at Veterans' Stadium to deal immediately with out-of-control or drunken fans. While the reputation—good and bad—of the Eagles-obsessed is well deserved, few American sports teams can claim fans with as much passion. (Go back to page 31.) ◀◀

*More than 68,000 fans cheer for their team, and taunt opponents, at every Eagles home game.*

# Pancreatic Cancer

The pancreas is a six-inch-long organ located in the abdomen, behind the lower part of the stomach. It is responsible for producing insulin, a hormone that regulates the body's use of glucose (sugar).

When cancer strikes the pancreas, the outlook for the patient is grim. Pancreatic cancer is highly aggressive and spreads rapidly. Overall, fewer than 5 percent of people with pancreatic cancer are alive five years after their diagnosis. Symptoms of the disease include upper abdominal pain, jaundice (yellowing of the skin and whites of the eyes), loss of appetite, and weight loss. In many instances, however, pancreatic cancer is already at an advanced stage before any symptoms appear. Only 10 percent of pancreatic cancers are detected while the cancer is still confined to the pancreas.

When the cancer is detected early, surgery is the best treatment option. Even so, only about 20 percent of the patients whose tumors have been completely removed will survive for five years. When the cancer has spread beyond the pancreas, surgery is useless. In such cases, the patient may be treated with chemotherapy, radiation therapy, or a combination of both. (Go back to page 34.) ◀◀

# Concussions

Cerebrospinal fluid, or CSF, is a clear fluid that surrounds the brain. CSF cushions the brain from shocks produced by bumps and blows to the head.

Sometimes, however, a trauma is forceful enough to propel the brain through the CSF and slam it against the inside of the skull. This is what causes a concussion.

In a concussion, there is a temporary interruption in brain function. This doesn't necessarily mean a person will lose consciousness. In fact, most people who suffer a concussion are not knocked out, and in many cases they aren't even aware of having sustained a head injury. Symptoms of concussion include headache, dizziness, nausea, and a dazed feeling. Usually, these symptoms go away within 7 to 10 days. The best treatment for a concussion is rest.

Athletes who sustain a concussion shouldn't return to the playing field before receiving a neurological examination from a doctor. They must also be completely free of symptoms. Someone who hasn't fully recovered from a concussion is at greater risk of suffering another concussion. Multiple concussions can lead to serious and permanent damage, including impaired mental ability. (Go back to page 42.) ◀◀

# The Pro Bowl

The NFL is the only major professional sports league that holds its annual all-star game after the regular season ends. Major League Baseball, the National Basketball Association, and the National Hockey League hold their all-star games in the middle of their seasons.

The first NFL-sponsored all-star game was played in early 1939, after the end of the 1938 season. The NFL champions, the New York Giants, beat a collection of all-stars from other NFL teams and two independent teams, 13–10. This version of the game, with the NFL champion playing a group of all-stars, continued for four years until World War II interrupted the NFL's play.

The all-star game resumed in 1950 and pitted the all-stars of the NFL's American Conference against the all-stars of the National Conference. After the NFL was realigned into East and West divisions in 1953, the game matched up the best players in the East with the best in the West. That arrangement continued until the NFL formally merged with the American Football League (AFL) in 1970. The game, now called the Pro Bowl, became a matchup between the best players in the AFC and NFC.

Three groups—the fans, players, and coaches—vote on who will play for the NFC and AFC in the Pro Bowl. Each group has one-third of the voting power to prevent fans of one team or one particular player from dominating the vote. Before 1995, only coaches and players were allowed to vote.

Starting in 1951, the Pro Bowl began giving a Most Valuable Player (MVP) award. From 1957 to 1971, the game presented two awards—one for the most valuable offensive back and one for the most valuable defensive lineman. One year later, two MVP awards were given, one to the best offensive player and the other to the best defensive player. Since 1973, however, only one MVP award has been given.

Some players look forward to the Pro Bowl as an opportunity for a postseason vacation. The game has grown into a weeklong celebration. The week before the game, there are numerous parties, an NFL alumni touch football game, a celebrity golf tournament, and a football skills contest.

From 1980 through 2009, the Pro Bowl was played at Aloha Stadium in Honolulu, Hawaii. In 2010, the game was held in Dolphin Stadium in south Florida. The date of the game was also changed in the 2010 season. The Pro Bowl used to be held a week after the Super Bowl, but in 2010 the game was played on the Sunday before the Super Bowl. This meant that players whose teams had reached the NFL's championship game would not be able to participate in the Pro Bowl. Some other players feel honored to be selected but choose not to play, so they can rest and recover from the long NFL season. (Go back to page 45.) ◀◀

**1986**  DeSean Jackson is born in Long Beach, California, on December 1.

**2001**  Enters Long Beach Polytechnic High School, where he becomes a star receiver and punt returner on the football team. Also is a standout in baseball.

**2004**  Named California's Mr. Football State Player of the Year. Named a high school All-American by *Parade Magazine*.

**2005**  Accepts a scholarship to play football at the University of California, Berkeley. Graduates from high school. Enrolls at Cal as a social welfare major. Leads the California Golden Bears in receptions, receiving yards, and receiving touchdowns in his freshman season.

**2006**  As a sophomore, returns four punts for touchdowns. Leads the nation in punt return average. Receives All-America honors from several organizations.

**2007**  Football stats decline, in part because of nagging injuries, though he still has a productive junior season.

**2008**  Announces in January that he won't return to Cal for his senior year but will enter the NFL draft. Is chosen in the second round of the draft, with the 49th overall pick, by the Philadelphia Eagles. Signs a four-year contract with Philadelphia worth just over $3 million. Has an outstanding rookie year, leading the Eagles in receptions, receiving yards, and yards per reception.

**2009**  Father, Bill, dies of pancreatic cancer in May. DeSean scores eight touchdowns before suffering a concussion against the Washington Redskins in the 11th game of the season. He misses just one game before returning to the lineup. Finishes season with 12 total touchdowns. His eight TDs of 50 or more yards ties NFL single-season record. Voted to Pro Bowl as wide receiver and kick return specialist.

## Career Statistics

| Year | Team | G | Rec | Yds | Avg | Lng | TD |
|------|------|---|-----|-----|-----|-----|----|
| 2008 | Philadelphia Eagles | 16 | 62 | 912 | 14.7 | 60 | 2 |
| 2009 | Philadelphia Eagles | 15 | 63 | 1,167 | 18.5 | 71T | 9 |
| Total | | 31 | 125 | 2,079 | 16.6 | 71 | 11 |

## Awards and Accomplishments

### High School:
**2004**   *Parade Magazine* All-American
Glenn Davis Award as Southern California player of the year
California Mr. Football Player of the Year
MVP of U.S. Army All-American Bowl

### College:
**2006**   First-team All Pac-10
Associated Press first-team All-America
Walter Camp Foundation first-team All-America
*Sporting News* first-team All-America
Football Writers of America first-team All-America

**2007**   All Pac-10 second team
American Football Coaches Association first-team All-America
Associated Press All-America third team

### NFL:
**2009**   NFC Special Teams Player of the Month (September)
NFL Offensive Player of the Week (October 26)
NFC Special Teams Player of the Week (December 13)
Selected to 2010 Pro Bowl

## Books

Didinger, Ray, and Robert Lyons. *The Eagles Encyclopedia.* Philadelphia: Temple University Press, 2005.

Gordon, Robert. *Game of My Life: Philadelphia Eagles—Memorable Stories of Eagles Football.* Champaign, IL: Sports Publishing, 2007.

MacCambridge, Michael, editor. *ESPN College Football Encyclopedia: The Complete History of the Game.* New York: ESPN, 2005.

Silverman, Steve. *The Good, the Bad & the Ugly Philadelphia Eagles: Heart-Pounding, Jaw-Dropping, and Gut-Wrenching Moments from Philadelphia Eagles History.* Chicago: Triumph Books, 2008.

## Web Sites

**http://www.nfl.com/players/profile?id=00-0026189**
DeSean Jackson's player page on the official Web site of the NFL provides recent and career stats for the Eagles wide receiver, game logs, video, and more.

**http://www.philadelphiaeagles.com/eagles_files/html/jackson_d_1.html**
The Philadelphia Eagles' media guide page on DeSean Jackson.

**http://www.pancreasfoundation.org/learn/pancreaticcancer.shtml**
The Web site of the National Pancreas Foundation contains information about pancreatic cancer.

**http://berkeley.edu/**
Read about DeSean Jackson's alma mater on the Web site of the University of California, Berkeley.

**double coverage—**in football, a tactic in which two defensive players guard one offensive player, usually a receiver.

**franchise—**the right or license granted by a company to an individual or group to market and sell its products.

**free agent—**a player who is not under contract to any team and who can therefore negotiate to play with any team he chooses.

**gridiron—**nickname for the field on which a football game is played.

**hand-eye coordination—**the ability to effectively process and use visual information in the performance of a manual task, such as catching a ball.

**mentors—**older, more experienced people who help teach or guide a younger person.

**minicamp—**a special, short training camp for football players that is usually held in the spring or early summer.

**practice squad—**a group of players who practice with an NFL team but aren't allowed to play in games; each team is allowed to keep eight players on its practice squad.

**protégé—**a person who is trained by, or whose career is furthered by, a more experienced or influential individual.

**showboating—**showing off.

**unsportsmanlike conduct—**in football, a personal foul called when, in the judgment of officials, a player taunts opponents or otherwise acts in a way that reflects poor sportsmanship.

**wild card—**one of two teams in each of the NFL's conferences that makes the playoffs without winning its division.

**page 7** "We were 8–8 . . ." Donovan McNabb, "Let's Get Some Weapons," *Yardbarker* blog, posted January 8, 2008. http://donovanmcnabb. yardbarker.com/blog/ DonovanMcNabb/Lets_Add_Some_ Weapons/63574

**page 12** "Oh, he pushed them . . ." Jennifer Allen, "In Spirit, Father of Eagles WR Continues to Inspire," *NFL Network.* http://www.nfl.com/ news/story?id=09000d5d810e38 6b&template=without-video-with-comments&confirm=true

**page 13** "A lot of my friends . . ." Allen, "Father of Eagles WR Continues to Inspire."

**page 13** "I had the craziest . . ." Allen, "Father of Eagles WR Continues to Inspire."

**page 14** "Football was important . . ." Nicole Lukosius, "NFL Moms See Football Values Firsthand," *USA Football*, October 21, 2009. http:// www.usafootball.com/articles/ displayArticle/7068/8392

**page 14** "They say you aren't good enough . . ." Bruce Feldman, "Born Identity," *ESPN The Magazine*, August 15, 2007. http://sports.espn.go.com/ espnmag/story?id=3618046

**page 17** "It was a mistake . . ." Feldman, "Born Identity."

**page 20** "About a week after . . ." Greg Biggins, "The DeSean Jackson Story," *Rivals. com*, February 3, 2005. http:// footballrecruiting.rivals.com/content. asp?CID=385490

**page 20** "About a week ago . . ." Biggins, "DeSean Jackson Story."

**page 24** "He is gifted . . ." "Eagles Take DeSean Jackson," *Phanatic Magazine*,

April 26, 2008. http://daily. phanaticmag.com/2008/04/eagles-take-desean-jackson.html

**page 26** "I think Coach Tedford just . . ." Feldman, "Born Identity."

**page 27** "I definitely think my junior . . ." Michael Bradley, "DeSean Jackson Is Ready for His Closeup," *Sporting News*, March 30, 2008.

**page 28** "He's slight of build . . ." Bradley, "DeSean Jackson Is Ready."

**page 29** "He has all the talent . . ." Associated Press, "Cal's Jackson Studying up for NFL Draft Under Rice's Tutelage," *NFL.com.* http://www.nfl.com/draft/st ory?id=09000d5d8072c48f&templat e=with-video&confirm=true

**page 31** "I thought I was in . . ." "DeSean Jackson Tries to Explain Screw-up," *FanNation*, September 17, 2008. http://www.fannation.com/truth_ and_rumors/view/67272

**page 36** "Everything about me in sports..." Jeff McLane, "DeSean Jackson's Father Passes," *Birds' Eye View: The Inquirer's Eagles Blog*, June 2, 2009. http://www.philly.com/philly/blogs/ inq-eagles/DeSean_Jacksons_father_ passes.html

**page 38** "This whole season . . ." Allen, "Father of Eagles WR DeSean Jackson Continues to Inspire."

**page 39** "more explosive plays . . ." Ashley Fox, "Eagles Show Some Explosiveness," *Philly.com Sports*, October 27, 2009. http://www.philly.com/philly/ sports/homepage/20091027_ Ashley_Fox___Eagles_ show_some_explosiveness. html?&subscribe=y&listID=1431

**page 39** "He's wicked fast." "Jackson's Two Touchdowns Lift Eagles over Sloppy 'Skins," CBS Sports.com, October 26, 2009. http://www.cbssports.com/nfl/gamecenter/recap/NFL_20091026_PHI@WAS

**page 41** "He was just a little . . ." Jeff McLane and Bob Brookover, "Eagles Notes: Concussion for DeSean Jackson," *Philly.com*, November 30, 2009. http://www.philly.com/philly/sports/20091130_Eagles_Notes___Concussion_for_DeSean_Jackson.html?&subscribe=y&listID=1431&action=login

**page 44** "He got us, man . . ." Associated Press, "Jackson Ties NFL Record for Long TDs as Eagles Get Shootout Win over Giants," ESPN.com. http://espn.go.com/nfl/recap?gameId=291213019

**page 44** "He loves playing . . ." Associated Press, "Jackson Ties NFL Record."

**page 44** "What makes you think . . ." Joe Drape, "Eagles' DeSean Jackson Balances Soft Hands with Sharp Talk," *New York Times*, January 8, 2010.

**page 45** "It's embarrassing . . ." Tim McMahon, "Dallas' Defense Stuns Jackson, Philly," ESPNDallas.com, January 10, 2010. http://sports.espn.go.com/dallas/nfl/columns/story?columnist=macmahon_tim&id=4812933

**page 48** "The main thing . . ." "One High School, So Many Future NFL Players," *USA Today*, April 22, 2008, p. 2C.

**page 51** "Jerry was a workaholic . . ." Ian O'Connor, "Rice Always Kept Faith in Dreams," *USA Today*, January 14, 2003, p. C3.

**page 51** "We're playing a game in . . ." O'Connor, "Rice Always Kept Faith."

**page 51** "balls dropped all over . . ." Damon Hack, "As Rice Pulls Down Passes, Time Seems to Stand Still," *New York Times*, January 12, 2003, p. H1.

**page 51** "I was very embarrassed . . ." Hack, "As Rice Pulls Down Passes."

Numbers in ***bold italics*** refer to captions.

**Seth H. Pulditor** is a longtime freelance editor. This is the first book he has written.

## PICTURE CREDITS

page